Berni Longobardi 200

THE LITTLE BOOK OF ZEN

HAIKU • KOANS • SAYINGS

Edited by Manuela Dunn Mascetti

Introduction by T. H. Barrett

BARNES & NOBLE
BOOKS
NEW YORK

This edition published by Barnes & Noble, Inc., by
arrangement with The Book Laboratory™ Inc.

2001 Barnes & Noble Books

M 10 9 8 7 6 5 4 3 2 1

ISBN 0-7607-2493-8

Contents

The word *zen* is the Japanese translation of the Chinese *chan* which in turn is the reading of the Sanskrit word *dhyan*, or meditation. Zen Buddhism is the path by which all dualistic distinctions like you-I, subject-object, are eliminated in meditation. The burning of duality is the ultimate Zen experience. Zen emphasizes the importance of this experience, of enlightenment or samadhi. In its unique style, Zen rejects religious practices and the intellectual study of doctrine as utterly useless in the realization of enlightenment, preferring other methods that allow to grasp enlightenment with an instantaneous shock of the ultimate truth.

Zen Treasures presents three of the traditional methods of Zen Buddhism: haiku, koan, and the sayings of the masters.

Haiku enlightens in the space of a breath. The shortest form of poetry in the world, a mere seventeen syllables in three verses, it is the length of a human breath. Haiku captures the Zen moment in its expressed form, and in this part of Zen Treasures are the traditional and modern haiku divided in the time-honored way according to the seasons. Poets included are Basho, Soseki, Kobayashi Issa, Dakotsu, Sogi, Busson, and also some American haiku poets.

Koans are the second traditional method of grasping enlightenment in Zen.

They are illogical conundrums, sometimes in the form of a phrase from a sutra, or an episode from the life of an ancient master, always paradoxical. Koans are an invitation to leap to another level of consciousness, where ultimate reality resides. They have been used in Zen as a systematic method of training since approximately the 10th century. By making clear the limitations of thought, the student struggles with a koan until an inner realization occurs that transcends dualistic thoughts. The realization of a koan is enlightenment. This section of Zen Treasures introduces the history, practice, and deep meaning of spiritual training and then presents a selection from the most traditional collection of teachings, The Gateless Gate and The Blue Cliff Records. The third and final part of Zen Treasures is dedicated to the antics of Zen masters, and includes stories from masters. These are potent stories that will instill the same Zen experience they did for the students living in monasteries long ago.

Zen Treasures includes the spectrum of Zen Buddhist wisdom enchanting the senses, enlightening the spirit, and initiating the mind. For the initiate and novitiate alike this is a beautiful offering of art and words that will plunge readers in a Zen moment on every page.

Manuela Dunn Mascetti

狩野

HAIKU

In the West "less is more" is a maxim that has only been articulated in our century, but the traditional Japanese practice of writing haiku shows that this principle has long been understood elsewhere. At seventeen syllables there is no room at all for error in its limited compass, but in the good haiku that is space enough for much more than may meet the eye at first reading. Perhaps this has something to do with the history of the poetic form, which only achieved its complete independence as recently as the nineteenth century, since by origin the haiku derives from an element in the Japanese "linked verse" composed by two or more authors, the meaning of whose lines might be radically modified by the next contribution in the sequence. But surely there is more to this than the mere fact that the haiku was first shaped to fit more than one context: surely in this "less is more" poetics there is no little hint of Zen?

There can be no doubt of this in the case of Basho, who famously described his itinerant, ascetic existence as "neither monk nor layman." But what, for example, of Buson, who seems to model himself much more on the image of the Chinese gentleman-poet? We should remember that over the thousand years or so that Chinese poetry had influenced Japan by his time, it was the Buddhist poets who were the most appreciated, and in the days when linked

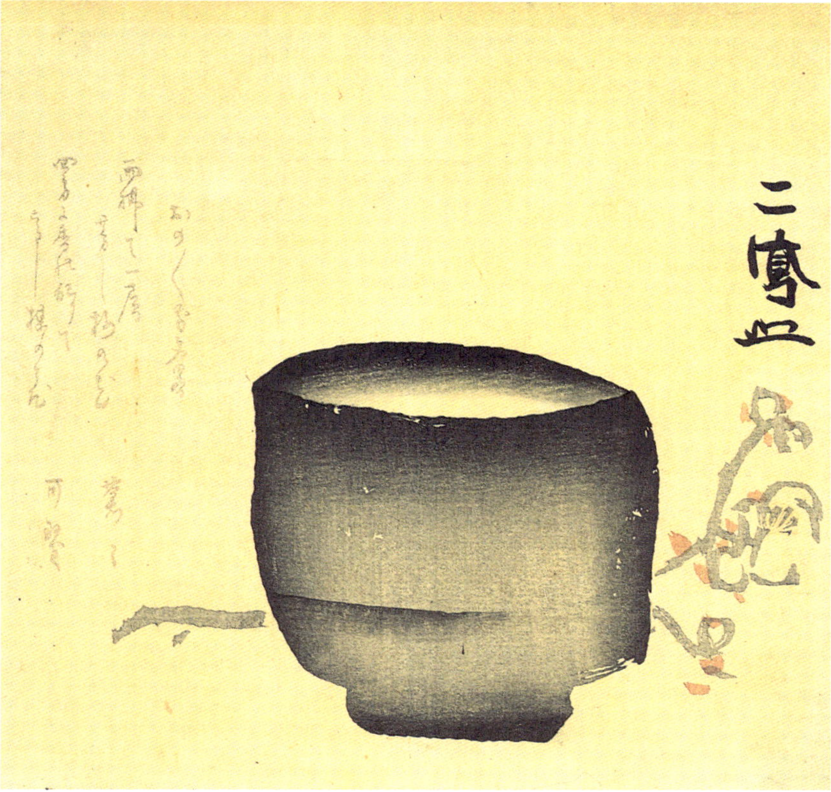

verse rose to prominence it was Zen monks who were responsible for diffusing a knowledge of continental poetry throughout Japan. The Chinese writers with whom the Zen monks were most familiar, for that matter, whether Buddhist or not, frequently drew analogies between poetry and Zen.

If, moreover, we trace such analogies back, it would seem that Buddhists of earlier times—when much Chinese poetry was inspired by heavy alcohol consumption—were concerned to propose as an alternative model of inspiration the heightened sense of reality achieved in meditation, no doubt very much to the advantage of East Asian poetry as a whole, and the haiku in particular. For though this form inherited an entire range of poetic conventions from earlier linked verse—from the use of season words to the format of the paper used to write the poem on—it still makes sense to speak of realism in the haiku, especially when the clear-eyed observation of ordinary life so typical of Basho plainly goes beyond anything in the more courtly environment of earlier poetry. And if, as the old Zen saying has it, "drawing water and carrying firewood" are the very activities in which supernatural power may be found, then we may well believe that it was not until the emergence of the haiku that this truth found its most telling realization in poetic form.

T. H. Barrett
Professor of East Asian History
School of Oriental and African Studies
University of London

The Art of Haiku

A monk once asked his Master, "No matter what lies ahead, what is the Way?" The Master quickly replied, "The Way is your daily life." This concept is at the very center of the Way of Zen. The principles that govern the Way are directed toward all of our existence, not just to the part that takes place in the meditation hall. The challenge of Zen is to meet each day, each moment with a clear mind and a cleansed spirit, so that the moment to moment union with existence becomes the highest teaching. This is the heartbeat that makes Zen today just as significant as when it was first brought from India to China by the wandering monk Bodhidharma in the year 520.

Zen has many flowerings, arts, and disciplines to which the Way (*do*) has been applied to create yet other forms of meditation and learning: *chado*, the way of tea; *kado*, the way of flowers; *kendo*, the way of the sword; *kyudo*, Zen archery; *judo*, Zen self-defense; *shodo*, Zen calligraphy. The underlying dynamism of all these arts is the full perception of the moment—being *here* and *now*—and this force is nowhere made more profound than in the subtle art of haiku.

Haiku is a poetic form which developed in Japan toward the closing of the seventeenth century. It consists of three phrases—or lines—of five, seven, and five syllables. Its popularity in Japan as a classic, and the enduring form in

which it is held in the highest esteem, lies in its nature and in the aesthetic principles that govern it. A haiku is like a vortex of energy; a haiku moment is a moment of absolute intensity in which the poet's grasp of his intuition is complete and the image he describes lives its own life. The art of haiku is to frame reality in a single instant that will lock the poet and the reader into sharing the same experience. It is this thunderbolt-like encounter that has made haiku the poetry of Zen—it is the voicing of those moments that cannot be described in prose or logic. This poetic form has breathing beauty and a moving elusive quality—reading it increases our sense of tranquillity and joy.

Haiku may be a more recent development of an extremely ancient form of Japanese poetry, called *katauta*, used to convey the utterances of the gods. The basis for *katauta* used to be the question-and-answer play of one god with another, which was reenacted by men and women at fertility and seasonal festivals. *Katauta* follows the same haiku pattern of 5-7-5 syllables, for a total of seventeen syllables, which is exactly the length of one human breath. The play between gods and spirits, thus, occurred in one breath, in one instant; and it is this same time frame that haiku has perfected to the ultimate art—the haiku moment. When we happen to see a beautiful sunset or lovely flowers we are often so delighted that we merely stand still. This state of mind might be

called "ah-ness" as we, the beholder, can only give a one-breath-long exclamation of delight: "Ah!" The object has seized us, we are being held, and we are aware only of the shapes, the colors, the shadows, and the blendings. In a brief moment we see a pattern, a significance we had not seen before. To render such a moment is the intent of all haiku, and the discipline of the form. Haiku poetry is a rendering of an experience, not a comment upon it. The closest approach toward a description of this art is to liken the process to the

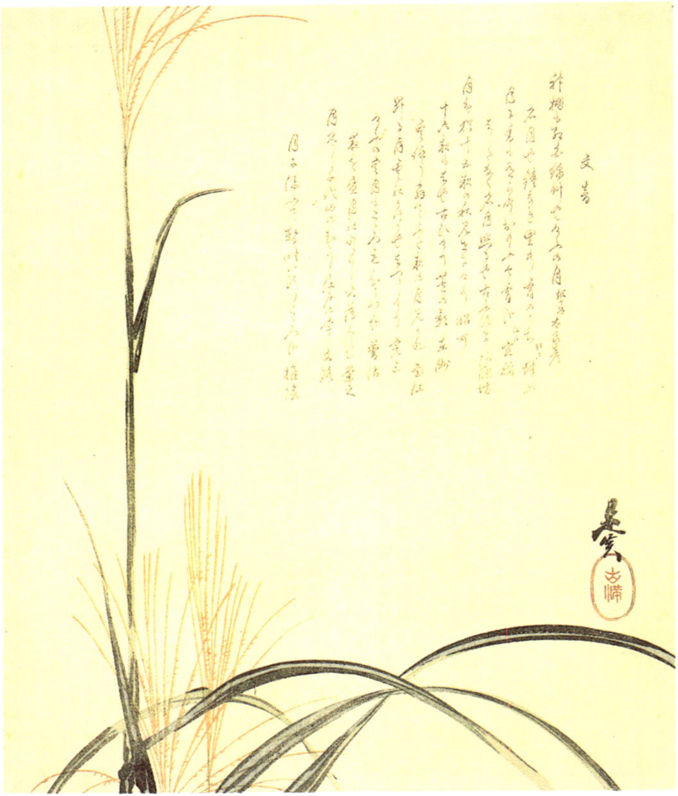

aesthetic appreciation of a painting in which contemplation and experience are one and the same consciousness. Every word in a haiku, rather than *contributing* to the meaning, like words do in a novel or sonnet, *is* an experience. Freshness is the flower of haiku art, for it is created by the immediacy of feeling. This gives the reader a true and everlasting delight; haiku can be read again and again without growing stale.

The haiku experience is made from three elements—where, what, when—which are bound in and with emotion to create a crystallized whole. In well-executed haiku, the elements of place, object, and time are so unified and so immovable that they create in the reader a nirvana-like sense. The key to understanding the skill of the poet is in the realization that in this art the artist strives always for the absolute. Of the absolute there is no question of degree; it is either attained or lost, just like a Zen experience. Most often it is not attained, and it is this constant striving toward and awareness of that high goal that has given strength to the aesthetic spirit that inhabits haiku.

Today in Japan, haiku is more popular than ever. The shortest form of poetry in the world is being adapted to our time and the wave of spiritual renewal it is bringing. Contemporary haiku reveals the skill of modern poets to remind

us of the traditional, and now slightly anachronistic, "old Japan" of tatami mats, bamboo flutes, and shrines dedicated to the gods, and, almost as polar opposite, of the new awareness and possibilities emerging in our fast-changing culture. Themes of light and shadow, sound and silence in modern haiku reveal a fascination with spatial sense and acceptance of universal forces in keeping with the formal traditions of an age now past. Other modern haiku poets, instead, break away from tradition by structuring their verses on anything other than the 5-7-5 syllabic form and by choosing themes unrelated to the natural world and the beauty of the changing seasons. As always, mastering the art of haiku takes years of practice. Japanese society considers that haiku poets do not attain maturity in this art until age 65, and many poets are well over 50 years old. Still, Japan has thousands of amateur haiku poets, and many experts in other professions write poetry as a hobby. A few thousand professional poets write, teach, appear on

TV and radio, and publish magazines. Haiku today has crossed the borders of Japan into the West and a few English poets and Zen adepts, especially in the United States, are attempting to compose verse by basing their work on the traditional Japanese form and content.

This volume presents selections from Matsuo Basho (1644–94), who was the first poet to develop the art of haiku, and his famed successors, Yosa Buson (1718–83) and Kobayashi Issa (1763–1827). These three are considered the first masters of haiku poetry. It also includes haiku by contemporary poets Natsume Soseki (1867–1916) and Toshimi Horiuchi, as well as classic verses by Hakuin, Ikkyu, Ryokan, and many other greats of the past. This volume further contains selections from contemporary Japanese women's poetry—Iida Dakotsu (b. 1914), Kimiko Itami (b. 1925), Sonoko Nakamura (b. 1913), Koko Kato (b. 1931), and Keiko Ito (b. 1935)—whose work is beginning to be translated into English for the first time. Not all the haiku selected for this volume follow the strict 5-7-5 syllable rule; these parameters were either lost in the translation from the original Japanese, or the poets decided to break away from this format and attempted innovation on the classical form. Haiku are inseparable from the changing seasons, and the poems in this book fall into the four traditional categories of spring, summer, autumn, and winter.

Spring

Covered with flowers
Instantly I'd like to die
In this dream of ours!

ETSUJIN

Sitting silently,
Doing nothing,
Spring comes,
And the grass grows by itself.

OSHO

In the rains of spring
An umbrella and raincoat
Pass by, conversing.

YOSA BUSON

The mother crow
Walks forward with her child
Following behind.

NARUSE OTOSHI

On the spring equinox
Clouds perambulate
Around the entrance of
a mountain temple.

IIDA DAKOTSU

Spring rain:
Come inside my nightgown,
You nightingale, too.

NATSUME SOSEKI

Like the sound of a fire crackling:
River snow,
Melting.

KEIKO ITO

With one another
Let's play; O sparrow
Who has no mother.

KOBAYASHI ISSA

How clear and sweet
The water of the mountain to
An evening pilgrim.

KAMIO KUMIKO

Amid the green broad expanse
Mount Fuji clouded over
By the spring storm.

MORI SUMIO

Plum flower temple:
Voices rise
From the foothills.

NATSUME SOSEKI

A single petal
Of the cherry blossom fell:
Mountain silence.

KENNETH TANEMURA

My mother's soul
Viewing the plum blossoms,
Returning at night.

NOBUKO KATSURA

Buddha Law,
Shining
In a leaf dew.

KOBAYASHI ISSA

What a long spring day!
Catching yawns from one another
We go each our way.

NATSUME SOSEKI

Brushing the leaves, fell
A white camellia blossom
Into the dark well.

BASHO

SUMMER

Under a blazing sky
A sail in the distance—
The sail in my heart.

YAMAGUCHI SEISHI

As I turn over
In the fresh smell of straw mat
Summer has begun.

YE QIAN-YA

Watch birth and death:
The lotus has already
Opened its flower.

NATSUME SOSEKI

"Summer thinness, dear,"
I replied to him and then
Could not check a tear.

KIGIN

Flickering campfire—
I kneel by the mountain spring
For a drink of stars.

CHARLES B. DICKSON

The lamp once out
Cool stars enter
The window frame.

NATSUME SOSEKI

Don't weep, insects—
Lovers, stars themselves,
Must part.

KOBAYASHI ISSA

A fractured rainbow
Is staining under thunder clouds with
Cathedral quiet.

JAMES KIRKUP

A red sun
Falls into the sea:
What summer heat!

NATSUME SOSEKI

Skylark
Sings all day,
And day not long enough.

BASHO

In the cicada's cry
There is no sign that can foretell
How soon it must die.

BASHO

My dead mother
Frequents my mind:
Wardrobe-changing season.

NATSUME SOSEKI

"Look, O look, there go
Fireflies," I would like to say—
But I am alone.

TAIGI

Where there are humans
You'll find flies,
And Buddhas.

KOBAYASHI ISSA

Are there
Short-cuts in the sky,
Summer moon?

LADY SUTE-JO

Weaving thoughts
Of cotton—
Summer solstice woman.

KIMIKO ITAMI

AUTUMN

On a withered bough
A crow alone is perching;
Autumn evening now.

BASHO

The wild geese take flight
Low along the railroad tracks
In the moonlit night.

SHIKI

Morning glory:
A beauty's charm
But a few days' dream.

NATSUME SOSEKI

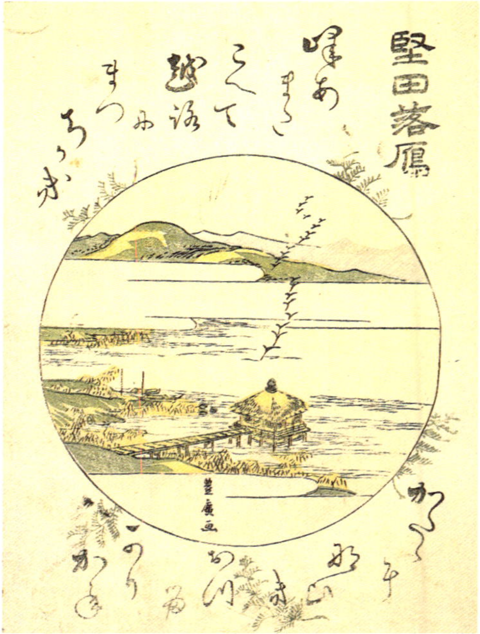

Full autumn moon—
On the straw mat,
Pine shadow.

KIKAKU

Autumn afternoon...
Without a ripple three white clouds
Cross the pond.

PATRICIA NEUBAUMER

Even the dumplings
Are smaller—
Autumn wind.

KYOROKU

Such a moon—
Even the thief
pauses to sing.

BUSON

O leaves, ask the breeze
Which of you will scatter first
From the verdant trees.

NATSUME SOSEKI

Fallen leaves—
Raking,
Yet not raking.

TAIGI

Autumn evening—
Knees in arms,
Like a saint.

KOBAYASHI ISSA

In the twilight gloom
Of the redwood and the pine
Some wisterias bloom.

SHIHOTA

Night frost—
Pulsing wings
Of mandarin ducks.

SOGI

A bell always rings
At dusk
In the water.

SONOKO NAKAMURA

Smell of autumn—
Heart longs
For the four-mat room.

BASHO

Storm—chestnuts
Race along
The bamboo porch.

SHIKI

The eyes of a stag
Listening to and feeling
Rising autumn wind.

FUKUDA KINEO

Wind in the West,
Fallen leaves
Gathering in the East.

BUSON

WINTER

Come, let's go
Snow-viewing
Till we're buried.

BASHO

Such silence:
Snow tracing wings
Of mandarin ducks.

SHIKI

Just by being,
I'm here—
In snow-fall.

KOBAYASHI ISSA

Not knowing why,
I feel attached to this world
Where we come only to die.

NATSUME SOSEKI

Wintry day,
On my horse
A frozen shadow.

BASHO

Through snow,
Lights of homes
That slammed their gates on me.

BUSON

Willow-trees are bare—
Dried the water, and the stones
Lie scattered here and there.

Buson

Cold, yes,
But don't test
The fire, snow Buddha.

Sokan

Living in the town
One must have money even
To melt the snow down!

Kobayashi Issa

Confined within doors
A priest is warming himself
Burning a Buddha statue.

NATSUME SOSEKI

Winter well:
A bucketful
Of starlight.

HORIUCHI TOSHIMI

At the winter solstice
The sun permeates the firmament
Of the mountain province.

IIDA DAKOTSU

See the river flow
In a long unbroken line
On the field of snow.

BONCHO

What is your
Original Nature,
Snowman?

NATSUME SOSEKI

Glittering flakes:
The wind is breaking
Frozen moonlight.

HORIUCHI TOSHIMI

Miles of frost—
On the lake
The moon's my own.

Buson

Outside the window, snow;
A woman in a hot bath
Overflowing.

Nobuko Katsura

Year's end—
Still in straw hat
And sandals.

Basho

KOANS

Now that the sound of "one hand clapping" has reverberated around our multicultural world, many people who have never undertaken Zen training have at least some idea of what a koan is. If asked, they would probably come up with a reasonable working definition, something like "a Zen riddle that defies logic," perhaps with a comment on the seemingly bizarre phrasing involved. Actually, the literal meaning of the word "koan" is somewhat unexpected: it signifies "a court case," or more concretely, "a file of legal documents." The very same word is even found in the titles of traditional Chinese detective stories, where, paradoxically, a puzzle-solving that is far from illogical is usually part of the plot.

But we must go back even further and consider the original context of the term. From the time of China's first emperor her rulers have administered the law through a bureaucratic hierarchy. A law court was a place of dread, and hell itself was popularly understood as another court of law writ large in the afterlife. To close the file of documents on a case, then, was not merely to solve a puzzle, but to resolve a matter of life and death—as much for the mandarin, with his superiors ready to scrutinize his every judgment, as for the poor unfortunates caught up in the legal process. What better word, then, for the documentation set before students of Zen, drawn from the words of earlier

enlightened masters? For how were such cases to be closed? There is no form of answer—verbal or nonverbal—that can possibly set aside such cases; the only possible form of closure is some form of enlightenment itself. We speak therefore of the study of koans as a system of education that would be shut down immediately by government inspectors in today's world: no curriculum; no time limit; above all, no success guaranteed, even to the committed and the intelligent.

True the Japanese Zen tradition has delimited a sequence of certain groups of koans to study out of a total of some 1,700—hence the Japanese pronunciation of names used here—but this is a purely notational arrangement. In practice, the original idea that a koan is no more than an expedient means toward entering the frame of mind of the former master to whom it is attributed has not been lost, and from this standpoint one koan is just as good as another. For what counts is not the answer but the answerer, so one

can well understand why the great Ta Hui is said to have burned his master's published koan collection for fear that students might read it simply as a training in repartee. Every educated person should be familiar with the classic koans included here, since their echoes resonate throughout subsequent East Asian Buddhism. But the original purpose of these stories was not education, not at all.

T. H. Barrett
Professor of East Asian History
School of Oriental and African Studies
University of London

The Zen Koan

Zen is the traditional temple life of Buddhist Japan and Korea. Originally, the beginnings of Zen Buddhism were brought to China by the Brahmin monk Bodhidharma, a direct spiritual descendant of Buddha's disciple Mahakashyapa, around the year 520. Though Indian teachers of various forms of Buddhism had preceded him, none had been able to establish a school or a line of disciples. Centuries before Bodhidharma brought with him the *essence* of Buddha's experience—his enlightenment. Casting away the traditional paraphernalia of Buddhism, its scriptures and deities, Bodhidharma succeeded in establishing a school in China where monks practiced the seated, cross-legged meditation advocated by him, and focused their goals not upon the learning of sutras, but upon the realization of their true nature. This practice was called *dhyana*—literally meaning "meditation" in Sanskrit—which was pronounced *Ch'an* in China and, later, *Zen* in Japan, where it eventually reached its full flowering and development.

The maturing of Zen out of the flower of Buddhism, however, was a gradual process. By the Middle Ages, Buddhism had become thoroughly assimilated into Chinese life. It was an institutional presence, with temples and monasteries a common sight in cities and countryside towns, and the monks and nuns wearing their traditional costumes formed a recognizable part of the population. With the widespread acceptance of Buddhism, the basic tenets of the religion had developed into a whole new spectrum of faith and ritual among the Chinese people who venerated and worshipped Buddhism but, dangerously, were not putting into practice its original and essential message. The task of early Chinese Zen masters was thus to bring Buddhist teaching to life in the here and now, and to show that enlightenment was not a superhuman goal to be achieved over eons of time, but a state of being that could be revealed through awareness in everyday life. In order to accomplish their role as transmitters of Buddha's original experience, Chinese masters invented a number of devices, such as koans, to give their disciples an immediate taste of Buddha's enlightenment.

What is a koan? This question must surely point us beyond the known and the unknown, to the unknowable.

Koans, literally meaning "cases," are a highly distinctive element in the history of Zen Buddhism, and there is no obvious parallel to them in the literature of any other religion. They are old Chinese-devised problems given to the Zen student for study—they are intractable, insoluble conundrums to which the disciple must find an answer. The answer, however, is not reached by any means of logic or thought; the answer is, rather, an experience, a realization. Most koans are based upon actual incidents in the lives of Zen masters and the activities of ancient monasteries. They are the answers of masters to their monks, or monks' questions to their teachers, and exchanges between enlightened masters. These are all men tremendously intent on being reborn, on satori. Their awakening through the practice of koans is one of the fundamental instruction methods of Zen. These tools, the result of spontaneous teaching, were recorded and handed down from monastery to monastery, generation to generation. Koans are used today for training students in all schools of Zen. Of the two major contemporary sects, the Rinzai places a greater emphasis upon koans, although the Soto sect uses them also.

Koans are a living memory of a time long past but still essential to our soul, when mind and logic did not rule people, but intuition and oneness with nature were the essential ways of expression and understanding. Koans are like resonating echoes of a part of ourselves that we need to call back to the surface in order to taste enlightenment. Koans are the art of turning to our own light and being illumined by it.

This book presents selections from the two major classic collections of koans—*The Gateless Gate* (*Mumonkan*) and *The Blue Cliff Records* (*Hekiganroku*). *The Gateless Gate* is the later of the two texts, having been composed in 1228 by the Zen monk Mumon Ekai, but it is usually studied first as it is shorter and has a simpler subject. *The Blue Cliff Records* were composed by Zen master Setcho (980–1052), and the book contains illusions and paradoxes of great subtlety and difficulty. This volume is organized according to koans of ascending difficulty accompanied by brief explanations to help the reader.

The genuine insight of such Zen masters as Ummon, Hyakujo, Baso, Joshu, Obaku, and Nansen into the essence of Buddha's message was the most crucial factor to the spreading of Zen throughout China and southern Asia. They were the experts who devised and propagated conceptual systems and forms of practice, and carried on the vital work of adapting the timeless teaching to the specific needs of times and places. They were the ones who communicated the dharma at the intimate person-to-person level, seeking out people whose sincerity and capacity made them suitable candidates to carry forth the torch of Zen. Analyzed as a body of wisdom, the koan collections presented in this volume form a careful and unique study of consciousness, and of the transformation of consciousness into wisdom. This is a map, charting the inconceivable, drawn by the ones who have been there for all of us who wish to follow.

The Gateless Gate

The great path has no gates,
Thousands of roads enter it.
When one passes through this gateless gate
He walks freely between heaven and earth.

Case 7—Joshu's "Wash Your Bowl"

A monk said to Joshu, "I have just entered this monastery. Please teach me."
"Have you eaten your rice porridge?" asked Joshu. "Yes, I have,"
replied the monk. "Then you had better wash your bowl," said Joshu.
With this the monk gained enlightenment.

Joshu (778–897), who attained full realization when he was seventeen years old, was one of the greatest Chinese Zen masters. By asking whether the young monk has already eaten his breakfast, Joshu is checking the monk's level of consciousness. The first daily practice of the monks in a Zen monastery is chanting sutras on a single low note, the vibration of which penetrates the body and the mind and prepares the monks for the absolute silence (*samadhi*) of the meditation that follows. Samadhi is maintained through a breakfast of porridge that is eaten solemnly. Perceiving the hidden meaning of Joshu's apparently practical question, the monk answers, *"Yes, I have,"* meaning that he was able to maintain samadhi while eating breakfast. Joshu's answer, *"Then you had better wash your bowl,"* is the Zen way of indicating to be here and now. The monk is no longer at breakfast; he should pay attention to the present. What is past is past; wash it away with the leftovers of the porridge.

Case 9—Daitsu Chisho Buddha

A monk asked Koyo Seijo, "Daitsu Chisho Buddha sat in zazen *for ten* kalpas *and could not attain Buddhahood. He did not become a Buddha. How could this be?" Seijo said, "Your question is quite self-explanatory." The monk asked, "He meditates so long; why could he not attain Buddhahood?" Seijo said, "Because he did not become a Buddha."*

Daitsu Chisho Buddha is the Buddha of Great Penetration and Perfect Wisdom. *Kalpa* is a measure of time, hundreds of thousands of years long. It stretches between the creation and recreation of a universe. Sitting in *zazen* for ten *kalpas* is a metaphor to show that in the state of absolute samadhi there is no time. In the state of samadhi there is no enlightenment, no realization, no Buddhahood; there is just this samadhi. Therefore, Daitsu Chisho Buddha did not *become* a Buddha because he *was* a Buddha from the beginning.

Case 15—Tozan's Sixty Blows

Tozan came to study with Ummon. Ummon asked, "Where are you from?" "From Sato," Tozan replied. "Where were you during the summer?" "Well, I was at the monastery of Hozu, south of the lake." "When did you leave there?" Ummon asked. "On August 25," was Tozan's reply. "I spare you sixty blows," Ummon said.

The next day Tozan came to Ummon and said, "Yesterday you said you spared me sixty blows. I beg to ask you, where was I at fault?" "Oh, you rice bag!" shouted Ummon. "What makes you wander about, now west of the river, now south of the lake?" Tozan thereupon came to a mighty enlightenment experience.

Ummon (d. 949) was the founder of one of the five major schools of Zen. Tozan (910–990) was one of the four most distinguished disciples of Ummon. To spare blows to a disciple is a great insult. The disciple is not even worth the punishment of the master. When Ummon asks Tozan what good his wandering from one monastery to another is, the master is revealing that what the disciple is seeking he already possesses. He should concentrate upon bringing it to the surface, rather than wandering here, there, and everywhere. At this realization Tozan attained enlightenment.

癸丑仲冬寫於寫山
樓中
文晁

CASE 19—NANSEN'S "ORDINARY MIND IS THE WAY"

Joshu asked Nansen, "What is the Way?" "Ordinary mind is the Way," Nansen replied. "Shall I try to seek after it?" Joshu asked. "If you try for it, you will become separated from it," responded Nansen. "How can I know the Way unless I try for it?" persisted Joshu. Nansen said, "The Way is not a matter of knowing or not knowing. Knowing is a delusion; not knowing is confusion. When you have really reached the Way beyond doubt, you will find it as vast and boundless as outer space. How can it be talked about on the level of right and wrong?" With these words, Joshu came to a sudden realization.

The ordinary Way is samadhi; it is peace of mind. When you are in samadhi, you are simply in samadhi; there is no searching after the Way. It is an experience, not a conceptual understanding. Samadhi is vast and boundless and beyond right and wrong.

CASE 21—UMMON'S "KANSHIKESTU"

A monk asked Ummon, "What is Buddha?" Ummon replied, "Kanshiketsu!"

Kanshiketsu, literally a "shit-stick," was used in old times instead of toilet paper. Shit-sticks become dirty to clean us. If this is not a Buddha, then what is? Out of gratitude to the stick, we call them Buddhas.

CASE 29—THE SIXTH PATRIARCH'S "YOUR MIND MOVES"

Two monks were arguing about a flag. One said, "The flag is moving."
The other said, "The wind is moving."
The sixth patriarch happened to be passing by. He told them,
"Not the wind, not the flag; mind is moving."

It used to be the custom of Zen temples that when a master was delivering a sermon, a flag was hoisted at the gate to announce it to the public. Two monks became distracted by the flag and started an argument. The sixth patriarch's remark led them to introspect into the nature of their minds.

Case 32—A Non-Buddhist Philosopher Questions the Buddha

A philosopher asked Buddha,
"Without words, without the wordless, will you tell me truth?"
The Buddha kept silence.
The philosopher bowed and thanked the Buddha, saying, "With your loving kindness I have cleared away my delusions and entered the true path."
After the philosopher had gone, Ananda asked the Buddha what the philosopher had attained.
The Buddha replied, "A good horse runs even at the shadow of the whip."

Buddha's silence—his samadhi—was the subtle lesson that the master taught to the philosopher. The subtlety of the teaching is like the shadow; the impact of enlightenment is the whip.

Case 38—A Buffalo Passes by the Window

Goso said, "A buffalo passes by the window. His head, horns, and four legs all go past. But why can't the tail pass too?"

"A buffalo passes by the window" is a metaphor for what happens during the practice of *zazen*. Thoughts, emotions, sensations all pass through consciousness as though they were clouds traveling across a clear sky. The head, the horns, and the four legs all go past: the activity of consciousness dies away when one enters samadhi during *zazen*. The tail, a metaphor for samadhi, can't pass because samadhi itself never passes away.

Case 40—Tipping over a Vase

Hyakujo wished to send a monk to open a new monastery. He told his disciples that whoever answered a question most ably would be appointed. Placing a water vase on the ground, he asked, "Who can say what this is without calling its name?" The chief monk said, "No one can call it a wooden shoe." Isan, the cooking monk, tipped over the vase with his foot and went out. Hyakujo smiled and said, "The chief monk loses." And Isan became the master of the new monastery.

The truth, here symbolized by the water vase, cannot either be told nor not be told; it can only be shown. Isan, a monk who studied with Hyakujo for twenty years, made a striking demonstration of this teaching.

Case 41—Bodhidharma's Mind-Pacifying

Bodhidharma sat facing the wall. The second patriarch stood in the snow. He cut off his arm and presented it to Bodhidharma, crying, "My mind has no peace as yet! I beg you, master, please pacify my mind!" "Bring your mind here and I will pacify it for you," replied Bodhidharma. "I have searched for my mind, and I cannot take hold of it," said the second patriarch. "Now your mind is pacified," said Bodhidharma.

Bodhidharma came from India to China around the year 520 and eventually settled in the kingdom of Wei where he practiced his "wall-gazing meditation" for nine years. The second patriarch, Bodhidharma's first disciple, was Eka. Legend tells that Eka wanted so badly to be taught by Bodhidharma that he cut his arm off in order to attract the attention of the master who was deep in samadhi. At this extreme gesture, Bodhidharma consented to help Eka pacify his mind by asking him to bring it to him. How can mind be brought anywhere? Eka, confronted with this request by the master, finds that he cannot get hold of his mind, much less bring it forth. The realization of no-mind brings immediate peace; the search for mind is frustrating until we realize that the search and the goal are one path leading to emptiness.

錦街若冲

CASE 46—PROCEED ON FROM THE TOP OF THE POLE

Sekiso Osho asked, "How can you proceed on further from the top of a hundred-foot pole?" Another eminent teacher of old said, "You, who sit on top of a hundred-foot pole, although you have entered the Way you are not yet genuine. Proceed on from the top of the pole, and you will show your whole body in the ten directions."

Sekiso Soen (986–1039) is here addressed as Sekiso Osho, the latter being a term of honor used for Zen masters. To be on top of a hundred-foot pole is a metaphor to indicate that Sekiso had attained a high level of consciousness, but he could not see how to proceed further. In the practice of meditation, one may come to a sort of extremity, to the brink at the edge of an abyss, where death is faced. This is a crucial moment in which a disciple might become panic-stricken. The elder master gives valuable advice to Sekiso; by hinting that he is not genuine, he indicates that, although Sekiso has attained a high level of consciousness, this condition is still measurable, bound, and not completely free from all attachments. The master wants Sekiso to go beyond the attachment to Buddhahood and samadhi. By proceeding on further from the pole, Sekiso will leave behind his attachments and attain complete freedom. *"You will show your body in the ten directions"* means freedom.

The Blue Cliff Records

Smoke over the hill indicates fire, horns over the fence indicate an ox. Given one corner, you grasp the other three; one glance, and you discern the smallest difference. Such quickness, however, is only too common among robed monks. When you have stopped the deluded activity of consciousness, then, whatever situation you may find yourself in, you enjoy perfect freedom, in adversity and prosperity, in taking and giving. Now tell me, how in fact will this sort of person behave? See Setcho's complications.

Case 3—Baso's "Sun-Faced Buddha, Moon-Faced Buddha"

The great master Baso was seriously ill. The chief priest of the temple came to pay his respects. He asked, "How do you feel these days?" The master said, "Sun-faced Buddha, Moon-faced Buddha."

Baso (709–88) was a peak in ancient Zen history. A total of 139 eminent Zen teachers had been his disciples. Baso's words "Sun-faced Buddha, Moon-faced Buddha" became one of the most famous sayings in Zen. Imagine being in the glorious presence of the setting sun at the far end of an ocean. Moment by moment the golden-faced Buddha sinks below the horizon, while, on the other side over the mountains, the moon is rising, inclined a little in her musing. It is in moments like these that everything is silent; the glory and the radiance bring us into absolute samadhi.

諸國名橋奇覧
山城あらし山 吐月橋

諸國瀧廻り
和州吉野
義経馬洗滝

Case 6—Ummon's "Every Day Is a Good Day"

Ummon addressed the assembly and said, "I am not asking you about the days before the fifteenth of the month. But what about after the fifteenth?
Come and give me a word about those days."
And he himself gave the answer for them: "Every day is a good day."

The days before the fifteenth of the month could be the days before today, or the days before you were born, or the days before your enlightenment. Ummon is not asking about what has happened before the present moment. "*What happens after the fifteenth?*" is Ummon's way of asking what happens to consciousness at this point in time and in the future. No one could answer Ummon, so he gave the answer himself—when you are in samadhi, every day is a good day, you don't ask about the past, nor wonder about the future. You are here, you are now.

Case 9—Joshu's "Four Gates"

A monk asked Joshu, "What is Joshu?"
Joshu said, "The East Gate, the West Gate, the North Gate, the South Gate."

Master Joshu came from a town also called Joshu, which was walled and had four gates, one in each corner. Joshu, the master, also has four gates—conversion to Zen Buddhism, training in *zazen* and koans, enlightenment in everyday activity, and the attainment of final nirvana. Joshu is indicating that anyone can pass his own gates and come for instruction. But unless a disciple has made progress through his training he cannot pass the gates; it is not Joshu who is blocking you, but you yourself.

諸國瀧廻り

Case 11—Obaku's "Partakers of Brewer's Grain"

Obaku addressed the assembly and said, "You are all partakers of brewer's grain. If you go on studying Zen like that, you will never finish it. Do you know that in the land of T'ang there is no Zen teacher?"
Then a monk came forward and said, "But surely there are those who teach disciples and preside over the assemblies. What about that?"
Obaku said, "I do not say that there is no Zen, but that there is no Zen teacher."

Obaku (d. 850) succeeded Hyakujo and was the teacher of Rinzai, founder of the Rinzai line of Zen. To be a partaker of brewer's grain has become a popular saying used to belittle all those who imitate Zen masters of old times. The meaning of these words is that you eat the grain left over by the brewers after they have made beer and then think that you are having a taste of the real thing. In stating that there is no Zen teacher, Obaku is reaffirming one of the strongest lessons in Zen—it cannot be taught. You must attain it by your own practice, study, and research.

CASE 14—UMMON'S "PREACHING FACING ONENESS"

A monk asked Ummon, "What is the teaching of the Buddha's lifetime?"
Ummon said, "Preaching facing oneness."

Zen masters deliver their sermons facing the image of the Buddha. However, the meaning of this koan is broader: oneness is absolute truth. To face oneness means to face every thing—yourself, the world, every being, and every thing—in its absolute truth.

富士三十六景
信濃塩尻峠

Sayings

Zen doubts over the value of writing would at first glance seem to be betrayed by the book you are reading now. Why more words, when verbiage obscures enlightenment like an entanglement of creepers smothering a living plant? But the true Zen master finds an equal obscurantism in silence: in the cause of enlightenment, the terse but telling phrase, compact enough to strike a spark, far outweighs any amount of dead letters or dumb silence. In Zen's Golden Age it was usually a fragment of living speech that set minds ablaze with a light that has shone through the centuries: that is why Zen sayings were valued then, and why they are valued now.

What strikes hardest and fastest is the simple utterance, as pared down as a line of poetry, and indeed one later writer observed that many Zen sayings constitute lines of poetry. No wonder then, that there are traces in early sources of the circulation of Zen anecdotes by word of mouth; like all outstanding communicators the Zen masters are best remembered (like the great wits of our own century) for their most pungent remarks; the spontaneity of religious insight in an age of doubt and despair would have struck home with particular force. For though the backdrop to the meeting described here of Yakusan and Rikoh—Yao-shan and Li Ao, in the Chinese pronunciation—is conventionally painted as one of rustic tranquillity, in reality the countryside harbored bandits or warlord soldiers, while the cities, too, had their gangs of hooligans. Immediate access to the truth was an urgent matter.

So transcripts of the masters' sayings, bristling as they were with colloquialisms shunned in polite literature, came to be esteemed as "Recorded Sayings," abiding reflections of their

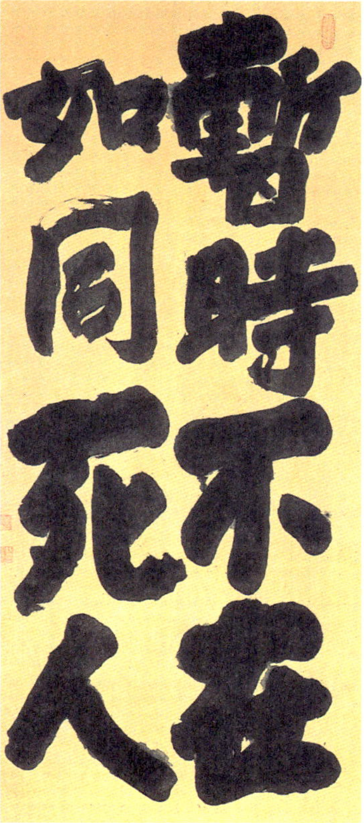

living presence. Whether Yao-shan and Li Ao have been reported verbatim I cannot say—the subtle interplay of character and dialogue suggests to me, at any rate, that their story has acquired a certain polish in being passed from hand to hand. Yet the Zen preference for commemorating the everyday and colloquial is clearly there from the start, and affects even later figures like Ta Hui who, while communicating in writing to his followers, retains a directness that speaks to us even today. For he, too, inhabited no idealized, misty landscape, but a world of sorrow and pain like our own, and many of his remarks confront directly death and loss in his community.

While some of these sayings are well over a thousand years old, there is no trace of the quaint or remote about them: rather our modern discourse seems trite and superficial by comparison. Whether these sayings convey enlightenment to us or not, they may at least teach us humility before the men and women of the past. What we do and say will surely be all but forgotten in a hundred—let alone a thousand—years, but here are words, plain words, that have stood the test of time.

T. H. Barrett
Professor of East Asian History
School of African and Oriental Studies
University of London

Zen Lines

Zen traces a unique lineage of enlightenment directly from Buddha. According to legend, the birth of the understanding of what was to become Zen occurred at a single moment of great significance in one of Buddha's discourses, "The Sermon on the Mount of the Holy Vulture." Buddha was preaching to a gathering of his disciples. He sat upon the podium and remained completely silent for a long time, and, instead of resorting to words in order to explain his point that day, he lifted a single lotus flower and held it in his hand for all to see. The disciples were baffled and could not understand the significance of his gesture, except for Mahakashyapa who quietly smiled at Buddha to show that he fully grasped the meaning of his gesture. Buddha, seeing his smile, declared, "I have the most precious treasure, spiritual and transcendental, which this moment I hand over to you, O venerable Mahakashyapa." Bodhidharma, who brought Zen Buddhism to China, was a direct spiritual descendant of Mahakashyapa.

Zen followers generally agree that this incident is the origin of their doctrine, for by raising the flower, Buddha symbolically revealed the innermost mind of Buddha-nature. The essence of Zen is revealed in what happened to Mahakashyapa, who, by letting the silence of the master penetrate to the very core of his being, understood its deep significance and attained enlightenment. The master is silent, the disciple smiles, the two minds are one. For the nearly two-and-a-half millennia that date the history of Zen, enlightenment has been the way of transmitting the message from one generation of Zen monks to the next. This direct line of experience resembles a transmission of the lamp that was first lit by Buddha so many centuries before. The sayings of the masters are thus an invaluable recording of wisdom traced through the centuries, wisdom that is as timeless as it is poignant and pertinent to us today.

Zen stories are known as *sutras*, a word initially used for the sermons of Buddha, but later also applied to the words exchanged between Zen masters and their disciples. Zen sutras present vivid pictures of the unimaginably vast, multilevel, intercommunicating reality experienced by the enlightened. The whole enterprise of the teaching and attainment of enlightenment is shown taking place in countless ways and among all manner of beings. The ordinary barriers of time, space, self, and other are transcended in these accounts of visionaries of the past. Zen sutras are perhaps the only existing chronicle, spanning over generations, of enlightened masters speaking. Sutras are a timeless treasure-trove in the extensive literature produced by the Zen school. Unlike the difficult koans, or the contemplative haiku, the sayings and stories of Zen masters are anecdotes of lives, facts, teachings, and events of real-life monks and nuns. As such, they are both ordinary and extraordinary and allow readers to view enlightenment within a down-to-earth context. What transpires from reading these chronicles is that the aim of Zen practitioners was not to escape from the world, but to achieve the kind of detachment and insight that would enable them to become immune to worldly entanglements. At the same time, it would allow them to function in the world with immense compassion, as they strove to bring enlightenment to others.

This book is a commemorative collection of stories, sutras, parables, proverbs, and sayings that run like a clear mountain stream from the past to the present to quench our spiritual thirst and cleanse our minds. One of the things that made Buddha's teachings so radical was his emphasis upon personal experience. In his sermons, Buddha repeatedly encouraged people to "come and see" for themselves, not to rely on scriptures, beliefs, or faith. Thus Zen developed its own unique contours and a set of beautifully tailored techniques for use in obtaining a direct experience of one's true nature—*satori* ("enlightenment" in Japanese).

Delightful, challenging, mystifying, mind-stopping, outrageous, and often scandalous, Zen is today the same soul-intriguing and totality-awakening experience as it was when Buddha reached enlightenment under the Bodhi tree. Zen has been a civilizing influence in Southeast Asia for centuries, and today it enriches and brings meaning to millions of lives, not only in Japan and Korea, but more and more to Western seekers who find sanctuary in the religion's simplicity and immediacy. At its core Zen is a diamond-hard way of attaining *religiousness* that has withstood the test of centuries and goes on shedding fragranced petals wherever it is established.

Reflections of a Zen Master

On Mindlessness

An ancient worthy had a saying: "To look for the ox, one must seek out its tracks. To study the path, seek out mindlessness. Where the tracks are, so must the ox be." The path of mindlessness is easy to seek out. So-called mindlessness is not being inert and unknowing like earth, wood, tile, or stone; it means that the mind is settled and imperturbable when in contact with situations and meeting circumstances; that it does not cling to anything, but is clear in all places, without hindrance or obstruction; without being stained, yet without dwelling in the stainlessness; viewing body and mind like dreams or illusions, yet without remaining in the perspective of dreams' and illusions' empty nothingness.

Only when one arrives at a realm like this, can it be called true mindlessness. . . .

"Just get to the root, don't worry about the branches."

Emptying this mind is the root. Once you get the root, the fundamental, then all kinds of language and knowledge and all your daily activities as you respond to people and adapt to circumstances, through so many upsets and downfalls, whether joyous or angry, good or bad, favorable or adverse—these are all trivial matters, the branches. If you can be spontaneously aware and knowing as you are going along with circumstances, then there is neither lack nor excess.

Ta Hui in a letter to Hung Po-Ch'eng

Tend the Ox

Since you are studying this path, then at all times in your encounters with people and responses to circumstances you must not let wrong thoughts continue. If you cannot see through them, then the moment a wrong thought comes up you should quickly concentrate your mental energy to pull yourself away. If you always follow these thoughts and let them continue without a break, not only does this obstruct the path, but it makes you out to be a man without wisdom.
In the old days Kuei Shan asked Lazy An, "What work do you do during the twenty-four hours of the day?"
An said, "I tend an ox."
Kuei Shan said, "How do you tend it?"
An said, "Whenever it gets into the grass, I pull it back by the nose."
Kuei Shan said, "You are really tending the ox!"
People who study the path, in controlling their thoughts, should be like Lazy An tending his ox; then gradually a wholesome ripening will take place of itself.

Ta Hui

The Inescapable

Whenever you run into something inescapable amidst the hubbub, you've been examining yourself constantly, but without applying the effort to meditate. This very inescapability itself is meditation: if you go further and adapt and apply effort to examine yourself, you're even further away. Right when you're in something inescapable, do not bestir your mind and think of examining yourself. The patriarch said, "When discrimination doesn't arise, the light of emptiness shines by itself." Again, Layman P'ang said:

In daily activities without discrimination,
I alone naturally harmonize.
Not grasping or rejecting anywhere,
Not going with or going against.
Who considers crimson and purple honorable?
There's not a spec of dust in the mountains.
Spiritual powers and wondrous functioning:
Hauling water and carrying firewood.
Just when you can't escape, suddenly you get rid of the cloth bag (of illusion) and without being aware of it you will be clapping your hands and laughing loudly.

Ta Hui

Discriminating Consciousness and Wisdom

Constantly calculating and making plans, flowing along with birth and death, becoming afraid and agitated—all these are sentiments of discriminating consciousness. Yet people studying the path these days do not recognize this disease, and just appear and disappear in its midst. In the teachings it's called acting according to discriminating consciousness, not according to wisdom. Thereby they obscure the scenery of the fundamental ground, their original face. But if you can abandon it all at once, so you neither think nor calculate, then these very sentiments of discriminating consciousness are the subtle wisdom of true emptiness—there is no other wisdom that can be attained....

This subtle wisdom of the true emptiness is coeval with the great void: the void is not subject to being obstructed by things, nor does it hinder the coming and going of all things within it.

Ta Hui

THE SAYINGS OF LAYMAN P'ANG

P'ang Yun was born in China in 740 and died in 808. Although he was a poor and simple man, he attained enlightenment as an ardent follower of *Ch'an* ("Zen" in Chinese). His timeless wisdom shows us that Zen is not a cloistered virtue cultivated by a few monks in remote monasteries, far and away from the daily toils of ordinary humanity. Zen is serenity and peace in every moment and action, and it is an open invitation to everyone. Layman P'ang, as he was known, was greatly admired by the Chinese, and even today his stories are used as teachings in many Zen schools.

Layman P'ang visited the great master Shih-t'ou to find out about Ch'an.
One day Shih-t'ou said to the Layman: "Since seeing me, what have your daily activities been?"
"When you ask me about my daily activities, I can't open my mouth," the Layman replied.
"Just because I know you are thus I now ask you," said Shih-t'ou.
Whereupon the Layman offered this verse:

> *My daily activities are not unusual,*
> *I'm just naturally in harmony with them.*
> *Grasping nothing, discarding nothing,*
> *In every place, there's no hindrance, no conflict.*

名勝八景

Who assigns the ranks of vermilion and purple?—
The hills' and mountains' last speck of dust is extinguished.
Supernatural power and marvelous activity—
Drawing water and carrying firewood.

Shih-t'ou gave his assent. Then he asked: "Will you put on black robes or will you continue wearing white?"
"I want to do what I like," replied the Layman.
So he did not shave his head or dye his clothing.
As the Layman and Sung-shan were walking together one day they saw a group of monks picking greens.
"The yellow leaves are discarded, the green leaves are kept," said Sung-shan.
"How about not falling into green or yellow?" asked the Layman.
"Better you tell me," said Sung-shan.
"For the two of us to be host and guest is most difficult," returned the Layman.
"Yet having come here, you strain to make yourself ruler!" said Sung-shan.
"Who doesn't!" retorted the Layman.
"True, true," agreed Sung-shan.
"To speak about 'not falling into green or yellow' is especially difficult," said the Layman.

"But you just did so," returned Sung-shan, laughing.

"Take care of yourselves," called the Layman to the group of monks.

"The monks forgive you for falling into activity," said Sung-shan.

At that the Layman went off.

The Layman was once lying on his couch reading a sutra. A monk saw him and said, "Layman! You must maintain dignity while reading a sutra."

The Layman raised up one leg.

The monk had nothing to say.

> *Not wanting to discard greed and anger,*
> *In vain you trouble to read Buddha's teachings.*
> *You see the prescription, but don't take the medicine—*
> *How then can you do away with your illness!*
> *Grasp emptiness, and emptiness is form;*
> *Grasp form, and form is impermanent.*
> *Emptiness and form are not mine—*
> *Sitting erect, I see my native home.*

ZEN ANECDOTES

Night Rain

Before he went to live in the mountains, Zen master Ranryo traveled throughout the four quarters, making no distinction between court and countryside, city and village, not avoiding even wineshops and brothels. When someone asked him why he acted in this way, the Zen master said,

"My Way is right there, wherever I happen to be. There is no gap at all."

Later Ranryo went into the mountains, where he built a simple hut and lived a life of frugal austerity as he continued to work on Zen.

Especially fond of night rain, Ranryo would burn incense and sit up on rainy nights, even until dawn. The people of the mountain villages, not knowing his name, used to call him "the Night Rain Monk." This amused him, so he began to use Night Rain as a literary name.

Once a visitor asked Ranryo about the relative merits of Zen meditation and the Pure Land Buddhist practice of Buddha-remembrance, reciting the name of the Buddha of Infinite Light. Ranryo gave his answer in verse:

> *Zen meditation and Buddha-remembrance*
> *are like two mountains;*
> *Higher and lower potentials*
> *divide a single world.*
> *When they arrive, all alike*
> *see the moon atop the peak;*
> *only pity those who have no faith*
> *and suffer over the climb.*

SOMETHING FROM NOTHING

Once on a journey Zen master Zenko happened to see a ruined temple that he thought should be restored. Completely without material resources of his own, Zenko wrote a large sign saying, "This month, on such-and-such a day, the pilgrim Zen master Zenko will perform a self-cremation. Let those who will donate money for firewood come watch."

Now Zenko posted this sign here and there. Soon the local people were agog, and donations began pouring in.

On the appointed day, people jammed the temple, awaiting the lighting of the fire. Zenko sat in the firewood, preparing to immolate himself. He called for the fuel to be ignited at his signal.

Now Zenko went into silent meditation. A long time passed. All of a sudden, he looked up at the sky and nodded. Then he addressed the crowd, saying, "Listen, listen! There are voices in the clouds! Just as I was about to enter into extinction, the saints all said, 'It is still too early for you to think of leaving the defiled world! Put up with this world for a while, and stay here to save living beings.' So I can't go on with the cremation today."

Then he took the money that had been donated and was able to restore the abandoned temple with it.

The Eleventh Hour

Chosha used to come to participate in the special annual intensive meditation session with Zen master Hakuin every single year, yet he never attained anything.

Finally one year Hakuin said to him at the conclusion of the session: "You come here every year, just like a duck diving into the water when it is cold. You are making a long journey in vain, without gaining half a bit of empowerment. I can't imagine how many straw sandals you have worn out over the years making this trip. I have no use for idlers like you around here, so don't come anymore!" Deeply stirred, Chosha thought to

himself, "Am I not a man? If I do not penetrate through to realization this time, I will never return home alive. I will concentrate on meditation until I die." Setting himself a limit of seven days, Chosha went to sit in a fishnet shed by the seashore. But even after seven days of sitting in meditation without eating or sleeping, Chosha was still at a loss. There was nothing for him to do but drown himself in the ocean. Removing his shoes in the traditional manner of a suicide rite, Chosha stood in the waves. At that moment, seeing the shimmering ocean and the rising sun merging into a crimson radiance, all at once he became completely empty and greatly awakened.

ZEN SUTRAS

Yakusan had not given a discourse for some time when, one day, the head monk came and said, "The congregation of monks are thinking about you preaching a sermon." Yakusan said, "Ring the bell!" The superior rang the bell, but when all the monks gathered, Yakusan went back to his room. The head monk followed him and said, "The master was going to give a talk, and the monks are all ready; why didn't you say anything to them?" Yakusan said, "There are sutra priests for the sutras, shastra priests for the shastras; why do you question my goings-on?"

Yakusan (751–834) became a priest at the age of seventeen and succeeded Sekito, becoming an outstanding Zen master. He established a monastery of great repute. He is one of the teachers mentioned in *The Blue Cliff Records*. This sutra shows the subtlety of Yakusan's teaching: although he agreed to give a talk, the talk itself was never given. That which needs to be said cannot be said, truth is a silent transmission. Yakusan deemed his monks mature enough to understand that sutra and shastra priests could expound on the dharma, but that the ultimate teaching has nothing to do with words.

In the days when Yakusan was still actively instructing his disciples, Rikoh—the governor of Ho-shu and also a great Confucian—went to visit

Yakusan, whom he greatly admired.
Yakusan was looking at a sutra when the attendant monk showed Rikoh into the master's room. Yakusan did not look up at the governor's arrival, but he appeared absorbed in what he was reading.
After a few moments, Rikoh, who had a hot temper, could not stand it anymore. He grumbled, "It's better to hear your name than to see your face," and stood up to leave.
Immediately Yakusan said, "Why do you respect the ear and look down on the eye?"
Rikoh pressed his hands together and bowed down. He then asked, "Could you please tell me what the Tao is?"
Yakusan immediately pointed up and then down with his hand and asked, "Do you understand?"
Rikoh said, "I don't understand."

冨嶽三十六景
凱風快晴

Yakusan shouted, "Clouds are in the sky; water is in the well!"
Rikoh suddenly realized and felt great joy. And with his contentment, he bowed down to Yakusan and presented this poem to him:

Achieved form, it looks like a form of the crane.
Under the thousands of pine trees, the way of the two poles.
I come and ask Tao: no wasteful argument.
Clouds are in the sky; water is in the well.

O*ne day, Tanka* [Tennen] *said to the monks who were with him, "You should all protect your essential thing, which is not made or formed by you. So how can I teach you to do this or not to do this?*
Once, when I saw Sekito Osho, he taught me that I should just protect it by myself.
This thing cannot be talked about. You all have your own zazen *mat; other than that, what Zen do you talk about?*
You should understand this. There is nothing which is to become Buddha. Don't just go on hearing the name of Buddha; you, yourselves, must see that the good devices and four infinite virtues are not from the outside; don't carry them in your mind.
What do you intend to follow? Don't use sutras.
Leave the emptiness without falling into it.
The seekers of the present day search for the Tao chaotically.

Here in this place, there is no way to learn, nor any dharma to show. Even a single sip or a single bite has its own truth.
Don't entertain thoughts and suspicions. In any place, the thing is present. If you recognize Gautama Buddha, an ordinary old man is that. You should all see, and get it, by yourselves. Don't let a blind man lead a mass of blind people into a fire cave.
If you play a dice game in the dark night, how can you see the numbers on the dice?"

Gyozan said to Sekishitsu, "Tell me what to believe in and what to rely on?"
Sekishitsu gestured across the sky above, three times with his hand, and said, "What do you say about reading sutras?"
Sekishitsu replied, "All the sutras are out of the question. Doing things that are given by others is dualism of mind and matter. And if you are in the dualism of subject and object, various views arise. But this is blind wisdom, so it

is not yet the Tao. If others don't give you anything, there is not a single thing. That's why Bodhidharma said, 'Originally, there is not a single thing.' You see, when a baby comes out of the womb, does he read sutras or not?
At that time, the baby doesn't know whether such a thing as Buddha-nature exists or not. As he grows up and learns various views, he appears to the world and says, 'I do well and I understand.' But he doesn't know it is rubbish and delusion. Of the sixteen ways or phases of doing, a baby's way is the best. The time of a baby's gurgle is compared to a seeker when he leaves the mind of dividing and choosing. That's why a baby is praised. But if you take this comparison and say, 'The baby is the way,' people of the present will understand it wrongly."

List of Color Plates

List of Color Plates

List of Color Plates

Haiku
Zen Haiku, Soiku Shigematsu, trans. and ed., Weatherhill, New York, 1994.
The Japanese Haiku, Kenneth Yasuda, Charles E. Tuttle Co., Inc. of Tokyo, 1957.
The Penguin Book of Zen Poetry, Lucien Stryk and Takashi Ikemoto, eds. and trans., Penguin Books, London, 1981.
A Long Rainy Season, Leza Lowitz, Miuki Aoyama and Akemi Tomioka, eds. and trans., Stone Bridge Press, Berkeley, 1994.

Koans
Zen Flesh, Zen Bones, Paul Reps, Charles E. Tuttle Co. Inc. of Tokyo, Japan, 1957.
Two Zen ClassicsThe Gatless Gate and The Blue Cliff Records, Katsuki Sekida, trans., Weatherhill, New York, 1995.

Sayings
Swampland FlowersThe Letters and Lectures of Zen Master Ta Hui, Christopher Cleary. New York: Grove Atlantic Inc.
Zen Antics, Thomas Cleary, Boston and London: Shambhala Publications, 1993.
A Man of Zen-The Recorded Sayings of Layman Pang, Ruth Fuller Sasaki, Yoshitaka Iriya and Dana Fraser, trans. Weatherhill, New York, 1992.

Aoyama, Shundo. *Zen Seeds—Reflections of a Female Priest.* Tokyo: Kosei Publishing Company, 1990.

Cleary, J. C., trans. and ed. *A Tune Beyond the Clouds.* Berkeley: Asian Humanities Press, 1990.

Cleary, Thomas. *Zen Antics.* Boston and London: Shambhala, 1993.

Osho. *Dogen, the Zen Master: A Search and a Fulfillment.*

——. *Isan: No Footprints in the Sky.*

——. *Joshu: The Lion's Roar.* Poona, India: Osho Foundation International.

——. *Ma Tzu: The Empty Mirror.*

——. *Nansen: The Point of Departure.*

——. *Rinzai: Master of the Irrational.*

——. *Yakusan: Straight to the Point of Enlightenment.* Poona, India: Osho Foundation International.

Sasaki, Ruth Fuller, Yoshitaka Iriya, and Dana Fraser, trans. *A Man of Zen—The Recorded Sayings of Layman P'ang.* New York: Weatherhill, 1992.

Manuela Dunn Mascetti is the author of *The Song of Eve, Saints, Goddess,* and coauthor with Peter Lorie of *The Quotable Spirit.* A Zen student of many years, she lives in London with her husband and her two Tiffanies named after Zen monks.

Professor Timothy Hugh Barrett, formerly Head of the History Department at the prestigious London School of Oriental and African Studies, is an expert on East Asian History who has studied Zen in both Japan and China for many years.